Dinosaurs and Their Discoverers™

Iguanodon and Dr. Gideon Mantell

Brooke Hartzog

The Rosen Publishing Group's
PowerKids Press™
New York

Published in 1999 by The Rosen Publishing Group, Inc.
29 East 21st Street, New York, NY 10010

First Edition

Book Design: Danielle Primiceri

Photo Credits: pp. 4, 5, 6, 9, 10, 11, 17, 18, 21, 22 © Linda Hall Library; p. 8 © American Museum of Natural History; p. 12 © 1997 Digital Vision Ltd.; p. 13 © 1996 PhotoDisc Inc.; p. 14 © Vince Streano/Tony Stone Images, Inc.

Hartzog, Brooke.
   Iguanodon and Dr. Gideon Mantell / by Brooke Hartzog.
         p. cm.—(Dinosaurs and their discoverers)
   Includes index.
   Summary: Tells how two amateur paleontologists, an English doctor and his wife, found a fossilized tooth that led to the discovery of a large species of dinosaurs known as Iguanodons.
   ISBN 0-8239-5325-4
   1. Mantell, Gideon Algernon, 1790–1852—Juvenile literature.   2. Mantell, Mary Ann—Juvenile literature.   3. Geologists—England—Biography—Juvenile literature. [1. Mantell, Gideon Algernon, 1790–1852. 2. Mantell, Mary Ann. 3. Geologists. 4. Iguanodon.] I. Title. II. Series: Hartzog, Brooke. Dinosaurs and their discoverers.
QE22.M32H37   1998
567.9'092—dc21   98-10337
                                                                                                        CIP
                                                                                                         AC

Manufactured in the United States of America

Contents

Digging Up Dinosaurs

As long as people have been on Earth, they have been finding dinosaur bones. Of course, people didn't always know that these bones once belonged to dinosaurs. When dinosaur **fossils** (FAH-sulz) were found in China thousands of years ago, people thought they were dragon bones. Some Native Americans who found dinosaur bones thought that giant animals had left their bones in the

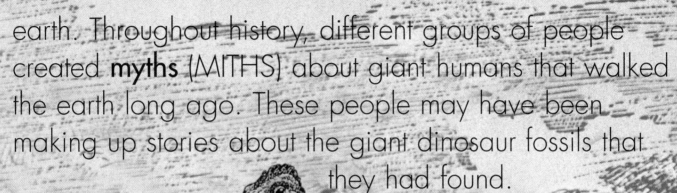

earth. Throughout history, different groups of people created **myths** (MITHS) about giant humans that walked the earth long ago. These people may have been making up stories about the giant dinosaur fossils that they had found.

◀ By studying fossils, scientists can learn about Earth's ancient animals.

Fossil Crazy

Millions of years ago, when animals and plants died, their remains would get covered by a layer of **sediment** (SEH-dih-ment). Over time the sediment became rock. When this happened, the remains of the plants and animals turned into fossils. People have always loved finding fossils. But people haven't always known that some of the fossils were dinosaur fossils. In the 1800s fossil hunting became very popular in Europe. Workers digging up the ground to build roads often found fossils. Families took trips to special places just to search for fossils. Scientists had begun to learn about Earth's history. But they still didn't know how dinosaur fossils fit into the picture.

At museums, people put fossil bones together into whole dinosaur skeletons for exhibits.

A Fantastic Find

In 1825 a very important fossil was discovered by Dr. Gideon Mantell and his wife, Mary. Gideon and Mary were **amateur** (AM-uh-chur) fossil hunters who lived in England. They were always looking for fossils in their spare time. One day Dr. Mantell was seeing a **patient** (PAY-shint) in his home office.

Dr. Mantell had a regular job, but fossil hunting was a hobby he enjoyed.

While Mrs. Mantell was taking a walk outside, she saw some rocks. The rocks had been dug up by workers who were building a road near her home. One rock looked strange. So Mrs. Mantell picked it up.

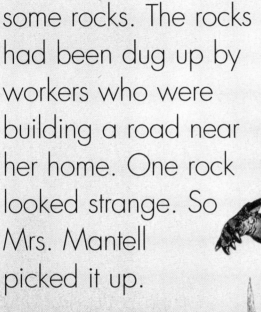

The Mantells' discovery turned out to be an important step in learning about iguanodons. ▶

What Is It?

The Mantells were very excited about what they had discovered. The rock they had found looked like a giant tooth. The tooth wasn't sharp. It was flat. It was a fossil. It reminded Dr. Mantell of an elephant's tooth. Elephants chew the plants they eat for a very long time. Over the years their teeth wear down and become flat.

But Dr. Mantell knew that elephants didn't live in England. This fossil was a real mystery!

It is hard to tell from just one fossil what the animal it came from looked like. The Mantells needed more information.

Solving the Puzzle

Dr. Mantell showed the giant fossil tooth to all the scientists he knew. One scientist thought it might be a fish tooth. Another scientist said it was a rhinoceros tooth. But no one was sure which animal was the right one. Finally Dr. Mantell took the tooth to a **museum** (myoo-ZEE-um) that had thousands of fossil **specimens** (SPEH-sih-minz). He hoped to find one that matched his fossil. He searched and searched. But there wasn't anything there like the tooth he'd found.

The scientists faced a puzzle. They had to put together the clues to figure out ▶ what kind of fossil they'd found.

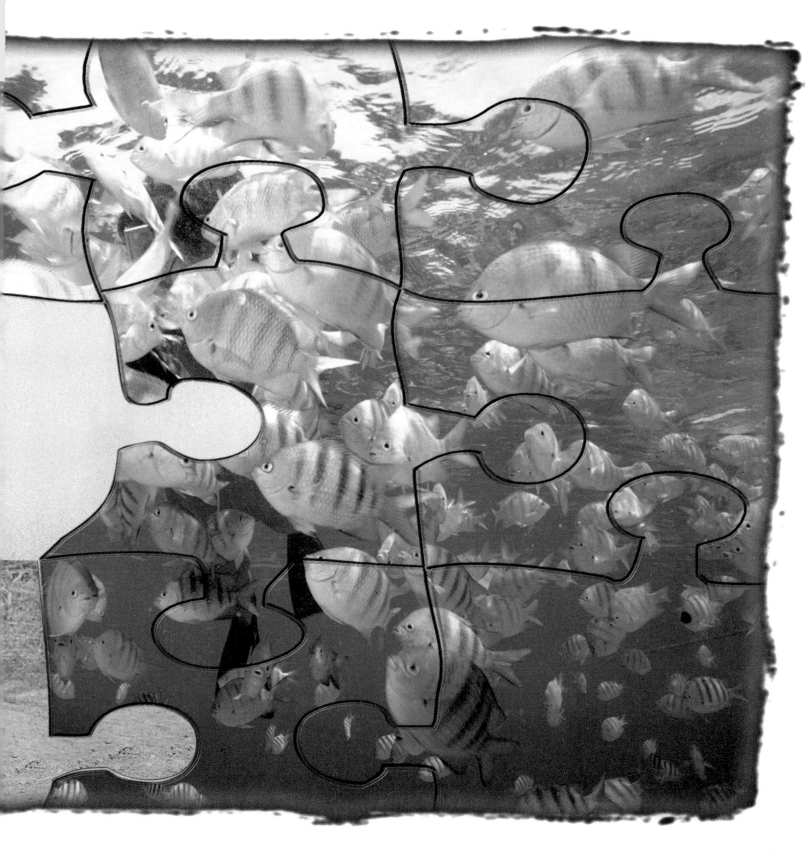

A Lucky Break

Just as Dr. Mantell was about to leave the museum, he met a young scientist named Samuel Stutchbury. He showed Samuel the strange tooth fossil. Samuel thought the tooth looked a lot like an **iguana** (ih-GWAH-nuh) tooth. But this tooth was much larger than most iguana teeth.

Samuel was an **expert** (EK-spert) on iguanas. He showed Dr. Mantell some other iguana teeth. They found two that were exactly like the fossil. Dr. Mantell finally had a clue that would help him and Mrs. Mantell. Now they just might figure out what kind of animal had left this tooth behind so many years ago.

◀ Studying modern animals, such as the iguana, can help scientists guess what animals from the past were like.

Naming Iguanodon

Over time Dr. Mantell found more teeth and bones in rock **quarries** (KWAH-reez). He believed these teeth and bones belonged to a giant **reptile** (REP-tyl) that had lived millions of years ago. Since its tooth looked so much like the iguana's, he named this creature **iguanodon** (ih-GWAH-noh-don), which means "iguana tooth" in Latin. But this reptile was different from many reptiles that live today. Dr. Mantell thought the iguanodon ate plants and was very large. He told other scientists that he thought the iguanodon was as big as a **locomotive** (loh-kuh-MOH-tiv).

At first scientists thought iguanodons walked on four legs. ▶

Dinosaurs Are Real

Dr. Mantell believed that huge reptiles had once lived on Earth and that they had all become **extinct** (ik-STINKT). Many scientists did not believe this. They laughed at Dr. Mantell. But ten years later, Dr. Mantell found hundreds of iguanodon **skeletons** (SKEL-uh-tuns) buried in one place. Soon other people began finding more and more giant reptile fossils. Scientists started to agree that Dr. Mantell had been right all along. A scientist named Richard Owen named the group of extinct reptiles dinosaurs.

◀ Dinosaur means "terrible lizard" in Latin.

The First Known Dinosaur

The iguanodon was not the first dinosaur that walked the earth, but it was one of the first dinosaurs that scientists discovered. Early ideas about the iguanodon and other dinosaurs didn't always turn out to be right. Dr. Mantell thought that iguanodons walked on all four of their legs, like lizards do. Later, scientists realized that iguanodons walked on two legs. At first, Dr. Mantell and other scientists thought that the iguanodon had a nose horn. Then they discovered the horn was really a large, sharp claw from an iguanodon's thumb. It takes scientists many years to fully understand a single discovery.

An iguanodon's thumb spike might have been used to grasp leaves to eat. ▶

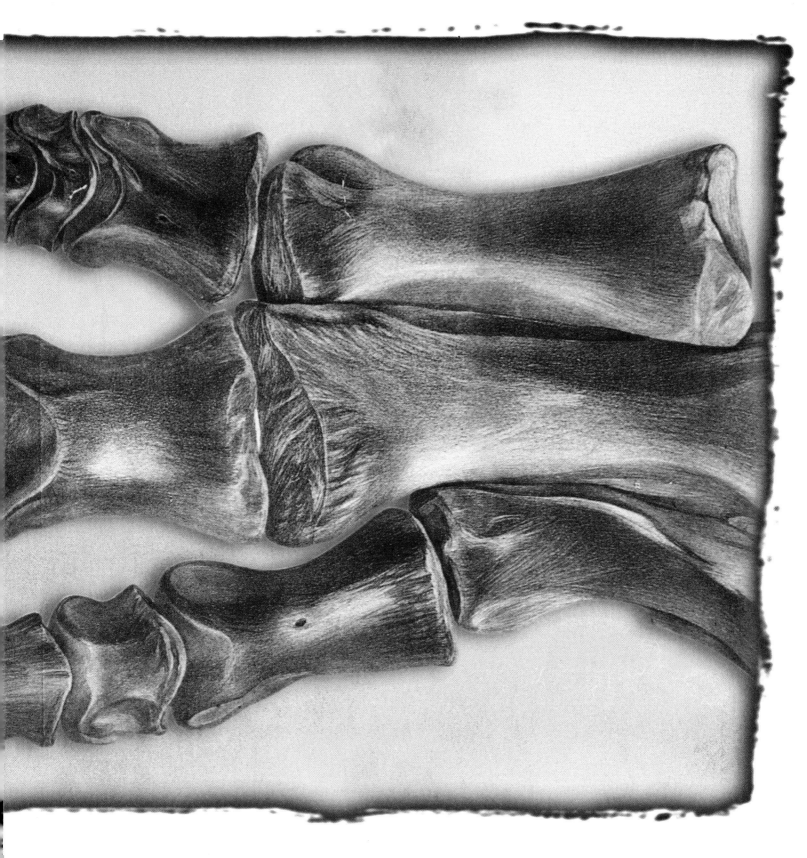

Dinner in a Dinosaur's Belly

Dr. Mantell died in 1852. He would have been very excited to see how interested people have become in dinosaurs. Children and adults want to learn as much as they can about dinosaurs. Many books have been written about dinosaurs. A **sculptor** (SKULP-ter) named Waterhouse Hawkins created life-sized models of the iguanodon and another dinosaur, the **megalosaurus** (MEG-uh-loh-SOR-us). Those statues still stand in a park in London, England. On New Year's Eve in 1853, a group of scientists had dinner inside the belly of the iguanodon statue.

Web Sites:

You can learn more about dinosaurs at this Web site:

www.questionmark.com.au/qm_web/dino.html

Glossary

amateur (AM-uh-chur) Someone who does something as a hobby, but not as a job.

expert (EK-spert) Someone who knows a lot of information about something.

extinct (ik-STINKT) To no longer exist.

fossil (FAH-sul) The hardened remains of a dead animal or plant.

iguana (ih-GWAH-nuh) A large lizard.

iguanodon (ih-GWAH-noh-don) A kind of dinosaur that looked like a lizard.

locomotive (loh-kuh-MOH-tiv) The first car of a train that pulls the rest of the cars.

megalosaurus (MEG-uh-loh-SOR-us) A giant meat-eating dinosaur.

museum (myoo-ZEE-um) A building where art or historical items are displayed.

myth (MITH) A story or legend used to explain events in nature or people's history.

patient (PAY-shint) A person getting care from a doctor.

quarry (KWAH-ree) A large hole dug in the ground from which stone is taken.

reptile (REP-tyl) A kind of cold-blooded animal, such as a lizard.

sculptor (SKULP-ter) A person who makes works of art in clay, metal, stone, or wood.

sediment (SEH-dih-ment) Gravel, sand, silt, or mud that is carried by wind or water.

skeleton (SKEL-uh-tun) The set of all the bones in an animal's body.

specimen (SPEH-sih-min) A sample.

Index